Westerlies

Kate Griffin

BookLeaf Publishing

India | USA | UK

Presentation by *BookLeaf Publishing*

Web: www.bookleafpub.com

E-mail: info@bookleafpub.com

ISBN: 978-93-5744-446-0

First edition 2022

DEDICATION

For all the people who are doing bigger and better things for the planet and the people that inhabit it. You rock.

ACKNOWLEDGEMENT

Thank you to my friends and family who continue to encourage me to write. Sorry for being so sappy. Love youse.

PREFACE

What is there to say that hasn't been said before? I hope to shed a tiny light on the simple, glorious minutiae of the everyday and the wanderings of the ancient rock we stand on.

Part 1

Breathe in. Breathe out.
Breathe in. Breathe out.

6000 kilometers to Antarctica,
You can still feel it's touch in the air.

Swaddled, bleary eyed and face to the horizon
Enviable naivety. Unadulterated hope. Pure joy.

The world is yet to touch you.
Hold it close and hold it tight.

Breathe in. breathe out
Breathe in. Breathe out.

Get ready, hold tight, and set sail!

Expectations

I expected something different,
I expected us to grow.

I expected to be fine,
I expected you to know.

To know what I was feeling,
To know that I was falling,
To know I wanted more,
Not be treated as a chore.

I know that you are smart,
Have a certain way with facts,
But indulgent ignorance is ugly,
And honey, that's your fact.

I was going to apologize,
For not speaking up sooner,
For letting this re run,
Go on and on and on.

But once I realized,
That my apology was nil,
I began to let go,
Let myself truly go.

What's that saying about insanity?
Should be the same for naïvety.

Look,

If only we could practice,
Practice what we preach.
Act out the lessons,
That you and I both teach.

See,

I'll make that first act,
Take that first leap.
I'm the one that's gonna,
Gonna get up and set sail.

I love you, I do.
But this time for me.
I love me, I do.
So this time,
I'm staying blue.

Summer

Remember that time,
Eating pies below blue summer skies?

Remember that time,
Burning your feet on summer concrete?

Remember that time,
South coast teens, matching jeans?

Remember that time,
Learning the stars, living in cars?

Remember that time,
Swimming in blue, one of the few?

But then,
Remember that one time…

Remember that one time
Your backyard was burning?

Remember that one time,
Your fortune was turning?

Red sky at night, shepherd's delight.

Red sky at dawn, the nation mourns.

Act now to survive.
Act now. To survive.
Act. Now. To. Survive.

Great Grandfather Magpie

Wake up.
Coffee.
Work.
Coffee.
Lunch.
Dinner.
Wine.
Sleep.

Wake up.
Coffee.
Work.
Coffee.
Lunch.
Wine.
Dinner.
Sleep.

Wake up.
Coffee.
Work.
Coffee.

Wine.
Lunch.
Dinner.
Wine.
Sleep.

Wake up.
Coffee.
Coffee.
Wander.
Great Grandfather Magpie.
Let's follow him for the day.
Sleep.

Wake up happy.
Coffee.
Work.
Coffee.
Lunch.
Dinner.
Wine.
Sleep soundly.

Living Through God Damned Clichés

The saying goes, or something so,
That absinthe makes the tart grow fonder.
But verse is cheaper,
You and I both know.

They say that ignorance is bliss,
To bury your head in the sand!
Scrap that mon amie,
Give me one more sweet sensuous kiss.

No use beating a dead horse,
Let sleeping dogs lie!
I'd rather not,
I'll scream around the whole course!

Good things come to those who wait,
Well, how long have you been waiting?
Waiting for this. Waiting for that.
Dangling a scraggly piece of bait.

Take the bull by the horns!
Full steam ahead!
Take off the gloves and let the claws come out!
It's one day at a time,
One foot in front of the other,
And take that road less traveled.

Hell no.

Be sure. Be loud. Be quiet. Be sure.
Be sure to inspect, retrospect, learn the dialect,
inflect, prospect, dissect, introspect!

Be whatever you want!
A prospector, a masticator, a mastibator, an
alligator, if you wish!

Above all else, watch those clouds,
Play, make believe, build a cubby under the
stairs.
And as the infamous They say,
Take the time to stop and smell the god damned
prose.

2021 Haven't Tried Sleeping

You have
All the time in the world.

It's up to you.

Plus,

It's going to be
Just as
Slow
For everyone one else.

I love you.

Poseidon's Children

The lion has its roar,
The religious, their lore:
We have thunder beyond the cliffs.

The magician has their tricks,
The salesman, their pitch:
We have the ocean's rhythm in our blood.

The worker has their debts,
The gambler, their debts:
We have the guttural call of the sea.

White horses charging through Lowers,
Bombies ploughing through Centres,
The peak smashing through The Bowl.

And The Button. That Button.
What does Lady Neptune have in store for you
today?

It's not a choice-
Not something we readily voice.
Not everything's a thing
That needs to be explained.

We are what we are:
Ocean Dwellers
Sea People
Poseidon's Children

Salty,
Animalistic,
Instinctual.
Grommet! Groveller! Shredder! Adventurer!

We will always choose the sea,
For that,
To us, is where
Our hearts will always be.

The Age of Entitlement

It is the Age of Entitlement,
But without the titles.

It is the age of technology,
But without the knowledge.

It is the age of auto-correct,
But without self-correction.

It is the age of tap, swipe, poke and like,
Without the feel, read, consider and need.

It is the age of advantageous opportunity,
With all its dumbfounded limitations.

With more on offer than ever before,
I feel more inadequate than ever before.

When does opportunity
Just become an indulgent privilege?

It is the "Age of Independence!"
They shout,
But I know they mean,
It is the Age of Mediocrity,
- Embedded Stupidity,
Governmental Insanity.

I hope I live to see the days:
Of Difference
Of Bioluminescence
Of Acceptance
Of Classic Grandpa Lance
Of Women Wearing Pants
Of Environmental Grants
Of Supportive Chants
Of not needing to take a bloody stance,
And just to be still.

To be still.

I wish I were a Tree

It would be so easy to be a tree
Standing up there, beyond the crap, free.

It would be so easy to be a tree,
Looking out high, seeing what there is to see.

But even trees crack and fall,
Brought down by a Southern Ocean squall.

But with every waxing of the moon,
Every guest on the breeze,
It believes it's where it needs to be,
Among its own, with other trees.

Pushing through the grass as a fragile, limber
sapling,
The path, Fates of Life, it's forever grappling.

So on it goes, just hoping and trusting.
That soon with knowledge and desire,
It'll be meaningfully gusting.

As the tree grows,
It yearns for the light

It believes in its roots, trusting they've found it right.

And so on it goes, growing taller and free,
Oh,
It would be so easy to be a tree.

Forever The Optimist

Every morning we wake,
Hoping for perfection.
More often than not, a silky lake.

Sometimes, wild and raw,
Every now and then,
Glassy, offshore.
But once in a while,
A breath draws in!
A rider! Fury and Style!
They paint the ocean's face,
Tempts her, embraces her,
With a caress and with grace.
And I watch with admiration,
With awe and fear,
As I look and hope,
For their entwined connection.

Again we wake,
Hoping for perfection,
But it's gone once more,
Welcome back: Bells Lake.

Praise be to He

He taught me to surf,
He taught me to swim.

The value of a fearless laugh,
I'm learning from him.

He taught me to read,
He taught me to ride:

I see in him,
Unwavering pride.

What can one give
In return for a compass?

Jus the trust and the love
That he has in his children.

The Fool

It is the fool who dares to foolishly fall in love.

For it is the fool's heart that is so damn foolishly
open and unwaveringly strong.

It is only us, The Fools, who have everything
But only us, The Fools, who have everything to
lose.

It is the Fool who stumbles and fumbles and
crumbles through their days;
They wander and ponder their way through their
foolish life maze.

It is the Fool's foolish friends who extend their
own foolish hands;
To grasp and grope and gather you up.

However, the Fool herself is not foolish.
She finds simple pleasures in:
The sun and the moon,
The sand and the birds,
The mountains and home.

For the Fool knows, home is where

Foolishness is welcomed and loved,
It is the Fool who dares to play,
Who so foolishly dares to love.

Rock on

21

I'd be attracted to a rock if it gave me attention.

Zen and the Art of Motorcycle Maintenance

Find poetry in everything.

Read everything because, who knows, your character may need it.

Will they be a scientist? If so, read an anthology of the human body.

Will they be a florist? Read a guide to native trees and plants in South America.

Will they be a teacher? Read a textbook that inspires you.

Read books that you hate. Read.

Natural Disasters

23

Natural disasters are only disasters because people live there. If an earthquake happens in a forest, does it constitute a disaster?

It's the same with affairs of the heart.

The Mother

The mother.

Mary. Barren. Separate. Hallowed. Pregnant.

Fingers of God. Stories. Life.

Love.

Caring, compassionate, guidance, listener.

Part of me, compass? Morality?

How can a heartbreak? It's muscle!

We must have two hearts!

Breakable.
Consumable.
A gift.

A Door

A door for the men.
A door for the priests.
A door for the women,
Separated by pillars, and more.

An eagle soars overhead,
Does enough to survey the features.

The church is guided by the sun.
Doors face east. Doors face west.

The girl is guided by the mother,
A compass for morality, for questions and
For answers.

Perfection

I saw a man pick a flower today.

What beauty.

I hope he has a good life.

What's for dinner?

Fear

How do you face fear, if it's fear itself that's facing you?

Do you sweet talk your way out of it?
Do you bribe him with an under the table sleight of hand?
Do you ignore him the way the moon ignores the sun on a winter's afternoon?

Fear is inevitable, predictable.
He's uncontrollable.
Unforgivable.

He is that toothache, blister on your heel.
He's the arthritis in your knee.
Annoying. And ever present.

Blank Pages

Blank pages.
New ages.

Blank faces.
Needing spaces.

New fears.
Old tears.

Trying to be true.
Trying to be strong.
Old fears, I thought I slew.
This feeling, I know it's wrong.

Wrong? Right?
But try I must,
With all my might,
To be strong and true,
These fears, I thought I slew.

New fears, old tears.
Warm wine, cold beers.
Blank faces, needing spaces.
Unheard words, leave no traces.

Part 2

Move on up, pack it in and set sail.
Use these winter swells to let your dreams
prevail.

Give out love, take it in and set sail.
Don't hesitate to care, don't hesitate to fail.

Create light, breathe it in and set sail.
Leave behind your burdens, let love guide your
trail.

Make me smile, hear me laugh, and set sail,
today!

Because one day the world we know will no
longer be out there. It will be in the person that
we meet, who is the world we want.

So set sail, set sail, set sail!
Become the world, create your own tale, and
with love my friend: set sail.